THINGS THAT FLY

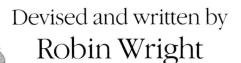

Devised and written by
Robin Wright

Designed and illustrated by
Teresa Foster

Edited by Tony Potter

Contents

About This Book	2
About Things That Fly	3
Making Things That Fly	4
Things You Need	5
Flutterby	6
Blow Dart Game	8
Corko Comet	10
Sky Diver	12
Whirly Peller	14
Whizzer	16
Tiler Glider	18
Astro Para	20
Rokka Chute	22
Patterns	24

About This Book

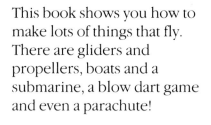

This book shows you how to make lots of things that fly. There are gliders and propellers, boats and a submarine, a blow dart game and even a parachute!

The pictures on this page show you all the things you can make.

Flutterby

Blow Dart Game

Everything is made from ordinary things that you might find around the house, like bags and pieces of packaging. There are lists of things you need on every page.

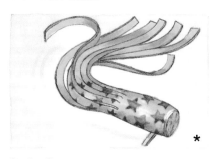

Corko Comet *

There are step-by-step instructions, and patterns at the back of the book to make it easy to draw any difficult shapes.

You might need help from a grown-up for things marked with a star like this: *

Sky Diver

Whirly Peller *

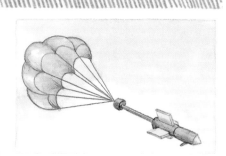

Rokka Chute

Astro Para *

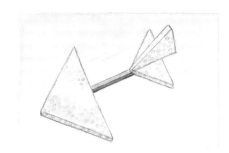

Tiler Glider

Whizzer *

About Things That Fly

◄ Things that fly either have to be lighter than air or overcome the force of gravity. Gravity is like a magnet – it is a force which keeps things on the earth's surface.

Things which are lighter than ► air will float on it, such as small feathers or thistle-down.

◄ Heavier things, such as planes, fly because their engines push them through the air and their wings lift them up.

Paper planes and other things ► you make are made to fly when you throw them through the air. Warm air floats above cold air. This is why hot air balloons work.

◄ Something which has tufts or a tail, like a dart, will float down to the ground. The tail acts as a brake which slows it down.

Parachutes catch the air. ► This slows down the parachutist so that he floats gently to earth.

Making Things That Fly

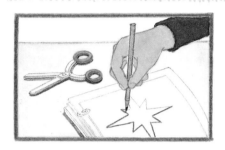

Photocopy or carefully trace the patterns at the back of this book. Cut them out with scissors.

Put things on a wooden board to cut them with a craft knife. Never cut directly on to a table.

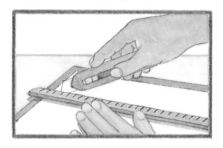

Be very careful when cutting with a craft knife. Use an old wooden ruler to cut against.

Always ask a grown-up to help you with anything you find difficult to do.

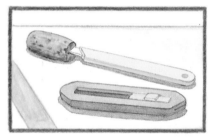

Push the craft knife blade into a cork when you finish. The blade on some knives goes back into the handle.

Try to be neat and tidy. Clear up tools and materials when you have finished working.

Make sure you wash out your brushes and replace lids on pots when you have finished.

Make sure that the glue and paints are dry before you try out the things you have made.

Test the things you have made by trying them out in an open space such as a park or garden.

Things You Need

You should be able to buy all these things from a craft or model shop, if you do not have them at home.

This page shows all the things you need to make the things in this book. It is a good idea to check with a grown-up to make sure it is alright to begin, and always ask if you need help with something.

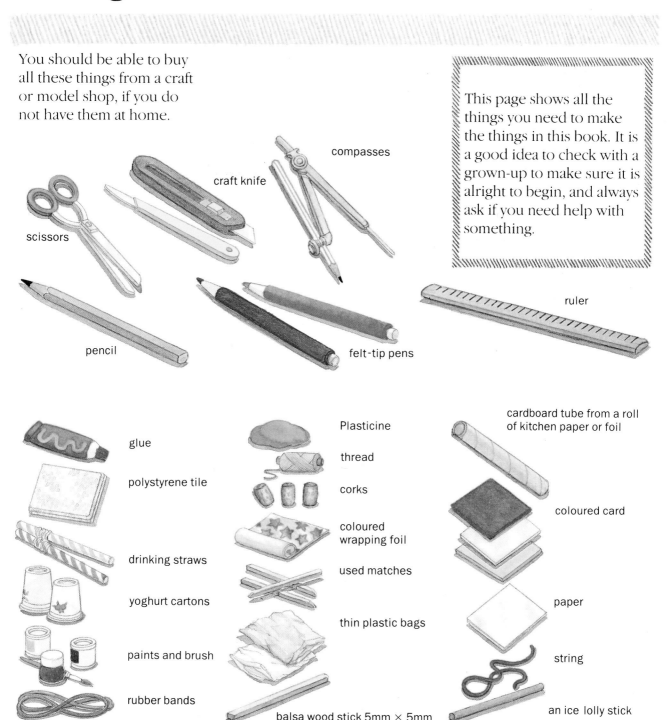

scissors

craft knife

compasses

pencil

felt-tip pens

ruler

glue

polystyrene tile

drinking straws

yoghurt cartons

paints and brush

rubber bands

Plasticine

thread

corks

coloured wrapping foil

used matches

thin plastic bags

balsa wood stick 5mm × 5mm

cardboard tube from a roll of kitchen paper or foil

coloured card

paper

string

an ice lolly stick

5

Flutterby

The Flutterby goes swirling round,
It's dizzy when it hits the ground.

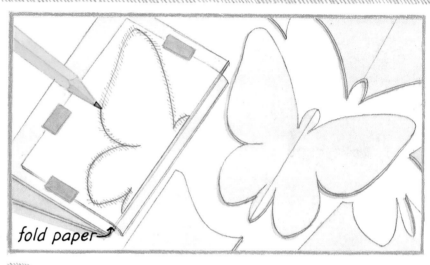

fold paper→

1 Fold a piece of paper in half. Trace the pattern on page 24 on to the folded paper.

Cut out the half shape. Unfold the paper to see the whole Flutterby.

What you need

paper

pencil

scissors

Plasticine

felt-tip pens

6   The pattern for the Flutterby is on page 24

bend wing tips

Plasticine

2 Colour the Flutterby with felt-tip pens. Put a small piece of Plasticine on the Flutterby's tail.

3 Bend the edge of one wing forwards, and the other wing backwards. This will make the Flutterby spin.

Why it works

When you throw the Flutterby in to the air, the Plasticine weight makes it fall tail first. The air pushes against the bent edges of the wings and makes them spin, rather like the propeller of an aeroplane.

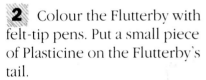

Blow Dart Game

*To blow the dart you need
some puff,
Are you sure you've got
enough
To make it fly from sky to
floor
And then to make a great big
score?*

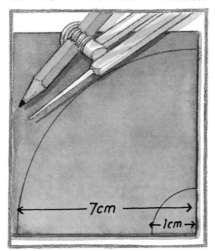

1 Make a quarter circle 7cm wide with compasses. Then make a smaller circle inside it, 1cm wide.

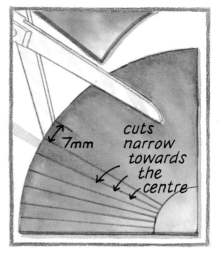

2 Cut out the big circle. Then make cuts about 7mm wide up to the line of the smaller circle.

What you need

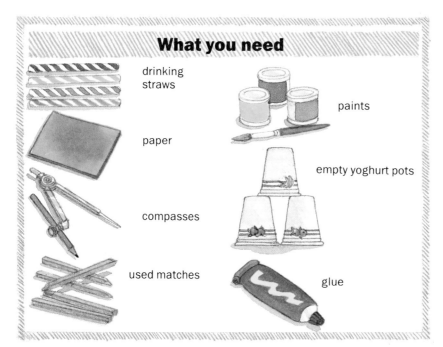

drinking straws

paper

compasses

used matches

paints

empty yoghurt pots

glue

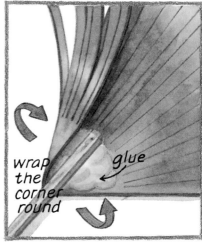

3 Put some glue on the corner of the paper, and wrap it round the end of a used matchstick.

fan out the cuts

4 Put the other end of the matchstick into a drinking straw; blow, and the dart will fly out.

5 Collect some empty yoghurt pots. Paint them and put a different number on each one.

How to play

Each player has three or four darts. The idea is to try and fire them so that the darts land in the pots. The number on the pot gives the score. The player with the highest score wins.

Why it works

When you blow into the straw, your breath is like a jet which forces the dart out into the air. The paper tail resists the air and makes the dart fall more slowly.

Corko Comet

Comets come and comets go,
That cross the sky, both to
and fro,
With sizzling tails and
starry trails
They sometimes make the
darkness glow.

ask a grown-up to do this

squeeze glue into the hole

1 Make cuts about 23cm long down one of the longer sides of the foil. Leave 5cm uncut at one end.

2 Make a hole in the cork. Do this very carefully with scissors. Put a drop of glue into the hole.

What you need

foil wrapping paper, 28cm × 8cm

a cork

an ice lolly stick

a rubber band

used matchsticks

cord or string, 20cm long

scissors

glue

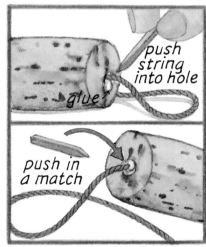

push string into hole

glue

push in a match

3 Insert one end of the string into the cork. Fix it by pushing in a sharpened matchstick.

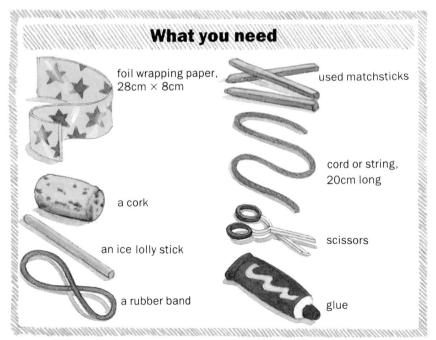

The pattern for the Corko Comet is on page 25

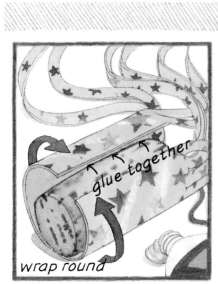

glue together

wrap round

4 Coat the sides of the cork with glue and wrap the foil round it. Glue one edge over the other.

push in and glue an angled match

5 Make a hole near one end of the cork. Glue in half a sharpened matchstick at a slight angle.

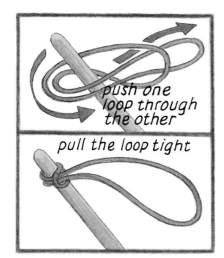

push one loop through the other

pull the loop tight

6 Tie the rubber band to the stick by looping one end through the other and pulling it tight.

Why it works

The rubber band and stick work like a catapult. Hook the angled match on the Corko Comet into the rubber band on the stick. Pull back the tail string, and let it go. The band stretches because it is elastic. When you let it go it flies back, sending the Comet into the air.

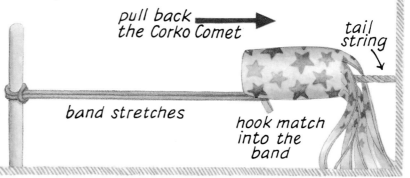

pull back the Corko Comet

tail string

band stretches

hook match into the band

11

Sky Diver

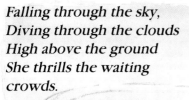

Falling through the sky,
Diving through the clouds
High above the ground
She thrills the waiting
crowds.

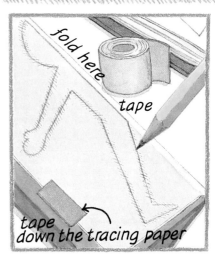

1 Fold the paper in half. Trace and draw the pattern of the Sky Diver on one side.

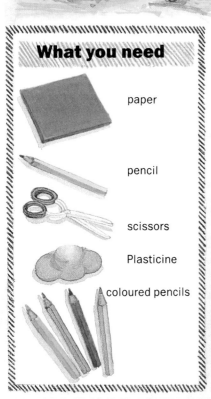

What you need

paper

pencil

scissors

Plasticine

coloured pencils

12   The pattern for the Sky Diver is on page 26

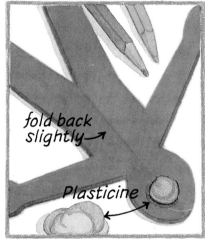

fold back slightly →

Plasticine

2 Cut out the Sky Diver, and unfold it. Draw in her face and clothes. Colour them with coloured pencils.

3 Stick a small piece of Plasticine about the size of a large pea on the back of the Sky Diver's head.

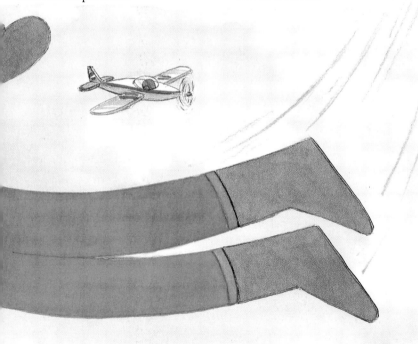

Why it works

If you hold the Sky Diver up above your head and let her go, she will glide gently down to the ground. She glides because her outstretched arms and legs make her float on the air. The Plasticine weight keeps her going forward, head first.

13

Whirly Peller

It spins like a top,
In the air, on the ground,
As your twist and flick
Sends it flying round.

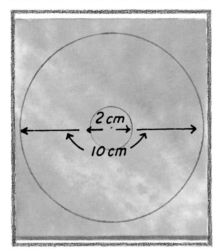

1 Draw a circle with the compasses set 5cm apart, then another with them set 1cm apart.

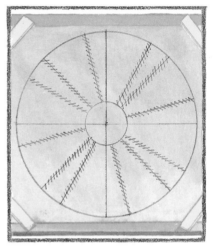

2 Trace and draw the pattern for the blades from page 27 onto the card.

What you need

thin card

scissors

pencil

drinking straw

ruler

compasses

glue

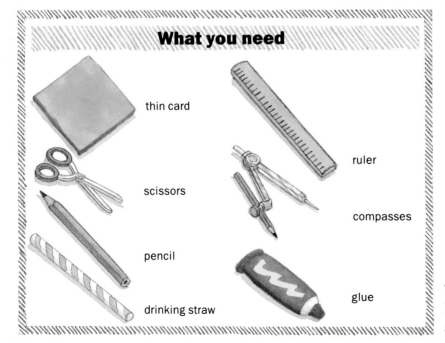

3 Cut out the card circle. Then carefully cut out the blades up to the edge of the small circle.

The pattern for the Whirly Peller is on page 27

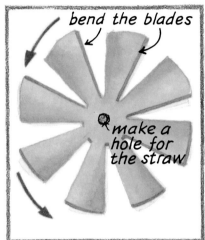

bend the blades

make a hole for the straw

4 Bend the left hand edge of each of the blades slightly, in the same direction.

glue

5 Make a hole in the centre of the circle with scissors. Push through about 10cm of a drinking straw and glue it.

Why it works

If you twist and flick the straw in your fingers, the Whirly Peller will spin through the air. The blades cut through air like an aeroplane's propeller.

15

Whizzer

It spins, it flies,
Through the air,
Across the skies.

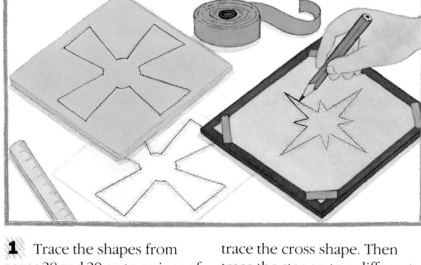

1 Trace the shapes from pages 28 and 29 on to a piece of tracing paper. Tape this to a piece of coloured card and trace the cross shape. Then trace the star on to a different piece of coloured card.

What you need

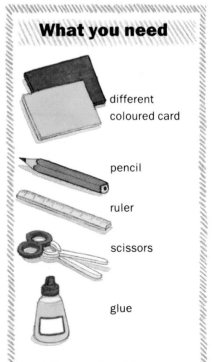

different coloured card

pencil

ruler

scissors

glue

2 Cut out the shapes. Use a craft knife for cutting out the spaces where the blades join the centre.

ask a grown-up to cut this part

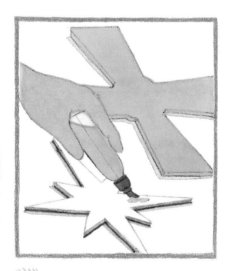

3 Glue the shapes together. Fit the spikes of the star evenly on and between the blades of the cross.

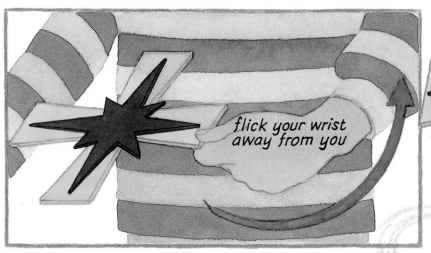

flick your wrist away from you

4 How to whizz it:
Hold the Whizzer by the end of one of its blades. Bring your arm across your body. Bend your wrist and then flick the Whizzer away from you. It works best if you keep it flat rather than at an angle.

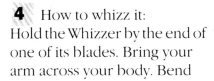

Why it works

The Whizzer flies through the air because of the force you use when you throw it. As it spins it cuts through the air in the same way as a propeller.

Tiler Glider

It swoops, it glides,
It rides the skies;
Like a bird it really
flies.

1 Measure a triangle with two sides each 16cm long. Draw a line across the tile as shown in the picture.

What you need

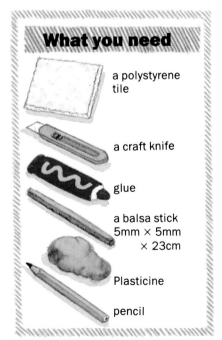

a polystyrene tile

a craft knife

glue

a balsa stick
5mm × 5mm
× 23cm

Plasticine

pencil

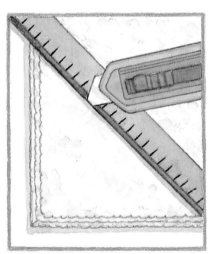

2 Using a ruler and craft knife, cut along the pencil line.

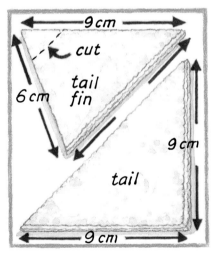

3 From the patterns and the measurements on page 30, cut the tail shapes from a piece of tile.

glue on tail fin

centre line of the wings

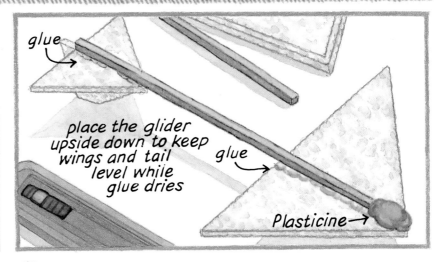

glue

place the glider upside down to keep wings and tail level while glue dries

glue

Plasticine →

4 Glue the tail fin to the tail. Carefully mark the centre line of the wings to fit the body.

5 Glue the wings and tail to the balsa stick body. Make sure they are straight and level. Stick a Plasticine weight on the nose.

The glider should just tilt forward when you hold it by its wing tips.

Why it works

The light wings and tail help the glider to lift and float in the air. The Plasticine weight keeps it balanced. Adjust the weight if necessary: too much will make it dive; too little will make it tail heavy.

19

Astro Para

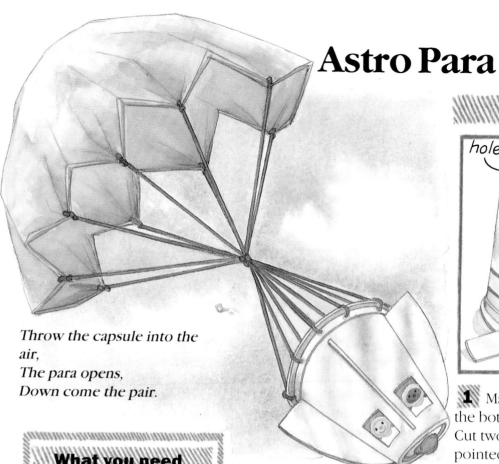

holes → *ask a grown-up to help cut out the windows*

holes

Throw the capsule into the
air,
The para opens,
Down come the pair.

1 Make nine holes round
the bottom and top of the pot.
Cut two windows with sharp
pointed scissors.

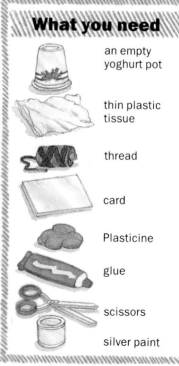

an empty
yoghurt pot

thin plastic
tissue

thread

card

Plasticine

glue

scissors

silver paint

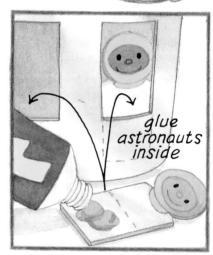

glue astronauts inside

2 Draw the astronauts from
page 31 onto card and cut them
out. Glue them behind the
windows in the capsule.

3 Cut nine 25cm lengths of
thread. Tie and glue each to
one of the holes round the top
of the yoghurt pot.

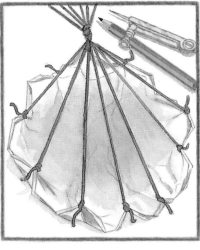

4 Pull all the threads together evenly. Then tie a knot in them half way up and put on a drop of glue.

5 Cut a 20cm circle from plastic tissue. Make nine holes round it. Tie and glue it to the threads.

Tuck the parachute carefully into the end of the capsule. Throw it up into the air nose first.

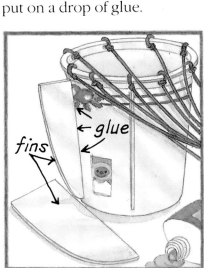

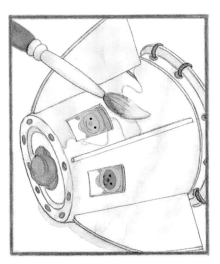

Why it works

When you throw the capsule air goes into the holes round the nose. This forces the parachute open and it fills with air. The open parachute acts like a brake, slowing down the fall of the astronauts.

6 Cut out the fins shown on page 31. Glue them to the sides of the capsule so that they are evenly spaced.

7 Paint the capsule and fins with silver paint. Stick a lump of Plasticine on the nose of the capsule.

Rokka Chute

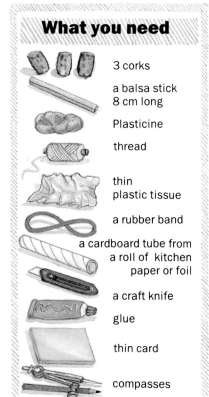

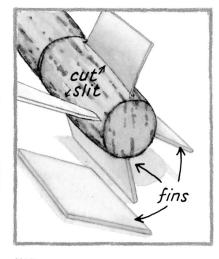

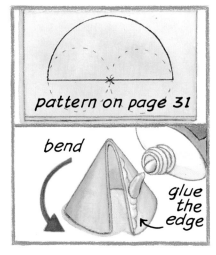

cut slit

fins

pattern on page 31

bend

glue the edge

1 Glue two corks together. Cut out the fins from card. Make slits in one of the corks and glue in the fins evenly.

2 Make a half circle of thin card twice the width of a cork. Cut it out and bend it into a cone. Glue the edges together.

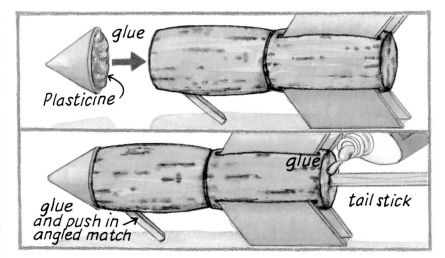

glue

Plasticine

glue and push in angled match

glue

tail stick

3 Fill the cone with Plasticine and glue it on. Push in and glue a sharpened matchstick at an angle. Make a hole in the tail end cork. Sharpen the end of the balsa stick. Glue and push the stick into the cork.

What you need

- 3 corks
- a balsa stick 8 cm long
- Plasticine
- thread
- thin plastic tissue
- a rubber band
- a cardboard tube from a roll of kitchen paper or foil
- a craft knife
- glue
- thin card
- compasses

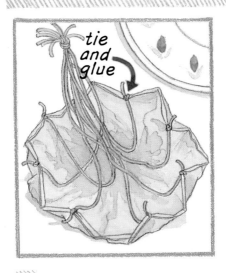

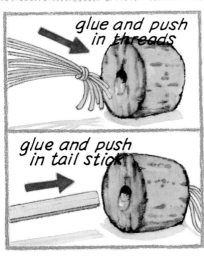

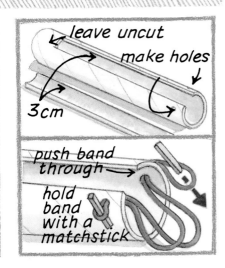

4 Cut out a 20cm circle of plastic tissue. Tie and glue eight 8 cm lengths of thread round it.

5 Cut 2cm from a piece of cork. Make a hole through it. Push in and glue the threads. Glue the other end to the stick.

6 Cut a 3cm wide strip from the tube. Make holes in the cut end. Fix the rubber band by matches and glue.

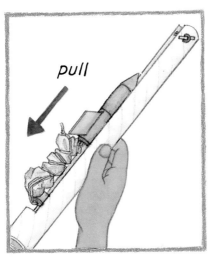

Why it works

7 Wrap the threads round the Chute. Rest and hold the Chute on the tail stick ready for launching.

8 Place the Rokka Chute in the tube, hooking the nose match over the rubber band. Pull it back and let go.

The rubber band stretches as you pull the Rokka Chute down the tube. When you let go, the band springs back because it is elastic. This forces the Rokka Chute up the launching tube. As it flies up, air fills the Chute and makes it open. The open Chute blocks the air and acts like a brake. This allows it to fall without being damaged.

23

Patterns

Flutterby

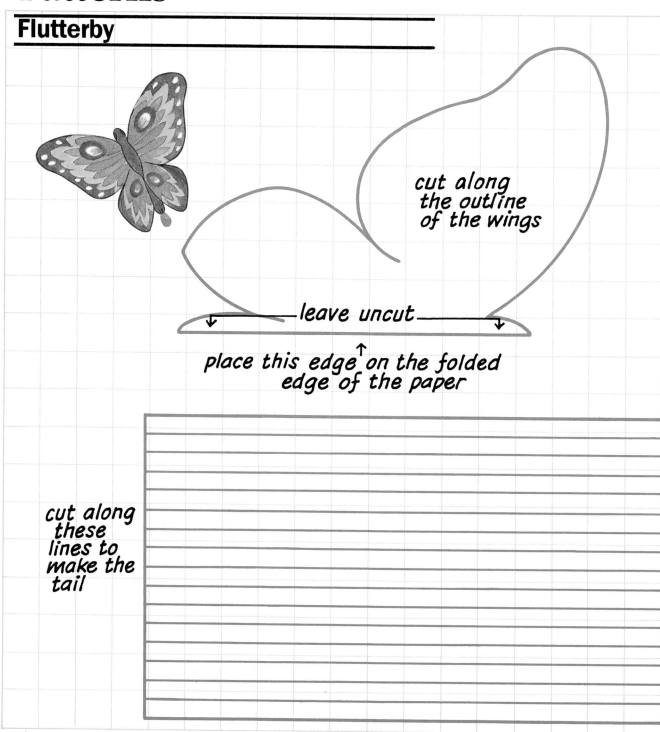

cut along
the outline
of the wings

leave uncut

place this edge ↑ on the folded
edge of the paper

cut along
these
lines to
make the
tail

Blow Dart Game

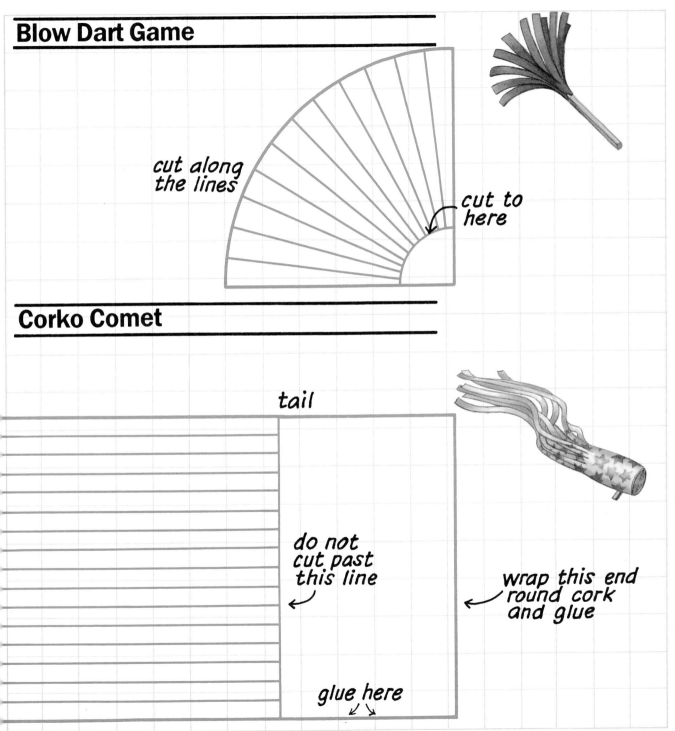

cut along
the lines

cut to
here

Corko Comet

tail

do not
cut past
this line

glue here

wrap this end
round cork
and glue

Sky Diver

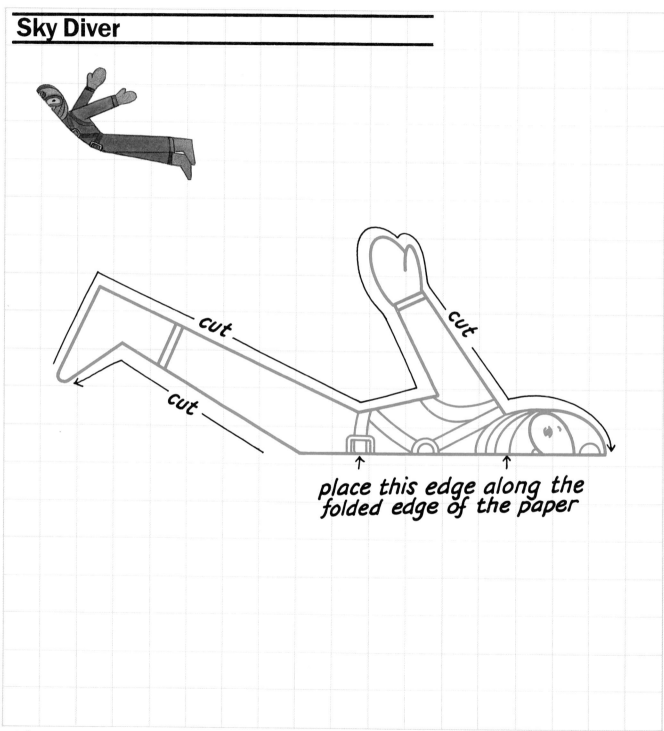

cut

cut

cut

place this edge along the
folded edge of the paper

Whirly Peller

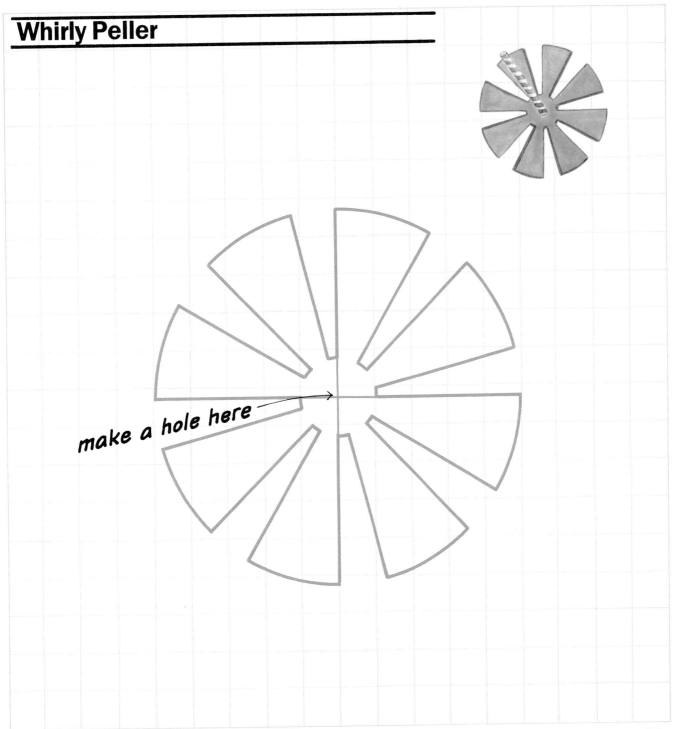

make a hole here

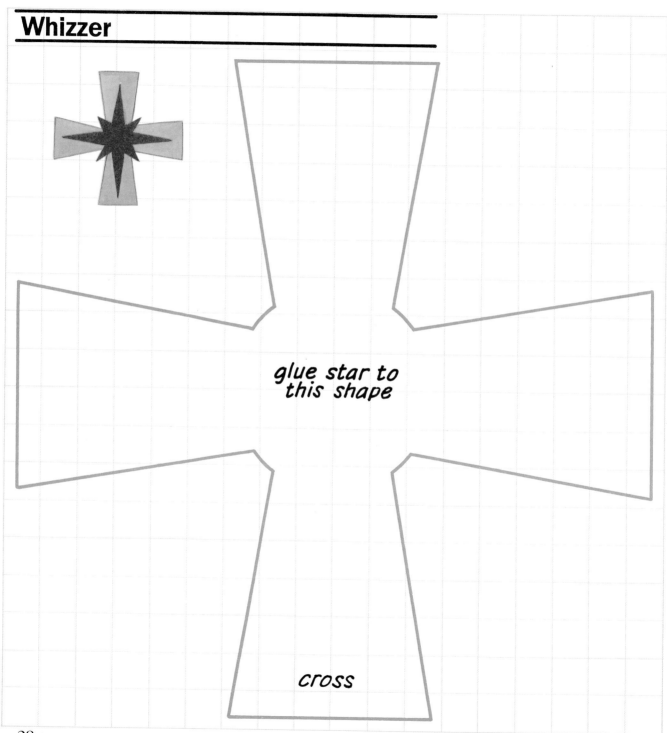

glue star to
this shape

cross

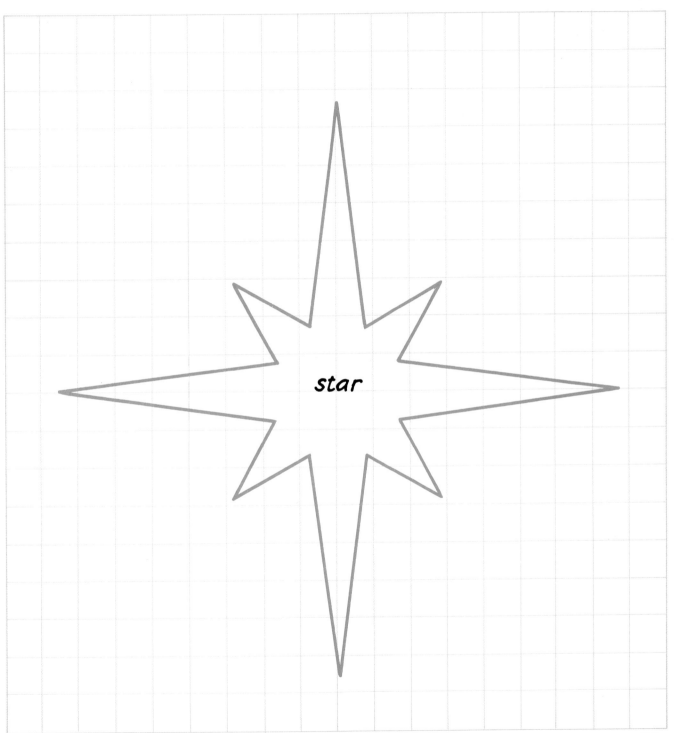

star

Tiler Glider

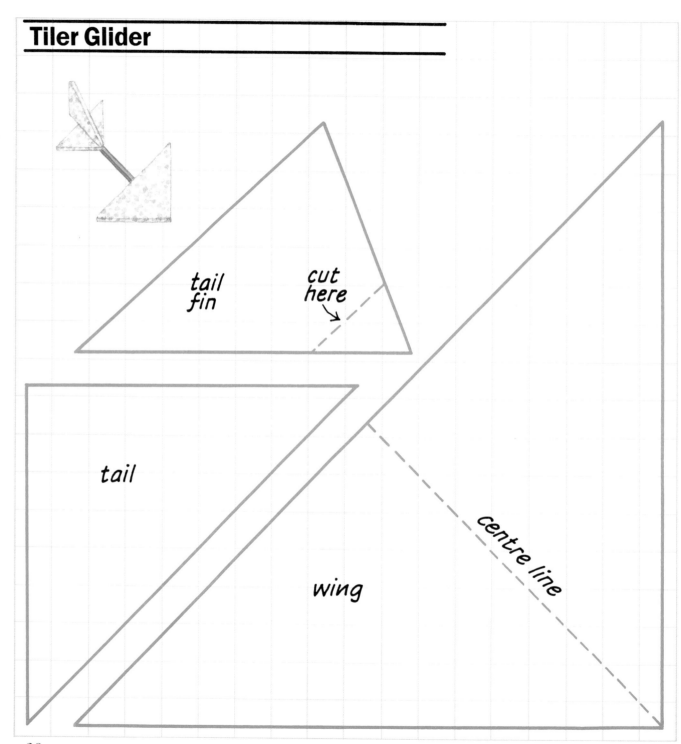

tail fin

cut here

tail

wing

centre line

Astro Para

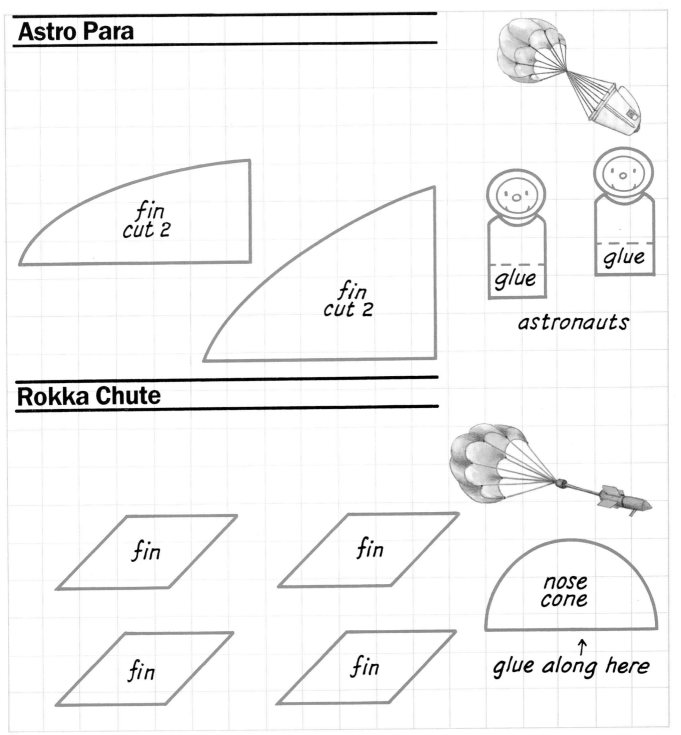

fin
cut 2

fin
cut 2

glue

glue

astronauts

Rokka Chute

fin

fin

fin

fin

nose
cone

glue along here

31

**Books are to be returned on or before
the last date below.**

LIBREX —

Printed in Portugal by Resopal